LET'S GO TO THE DESERT

HARRIET E. HUNTINGTON

LET'S GO TO THE DESERT

ILLUSTRATED WITH PHOTOGRAPHS BY THE AUTHOR

JUNIOR BOOKS DOUBLEDAY & COMPANY, INC., GARDEN CITY, N. Y., 1949

PRINTED IN THE UNITED STATES OF AMERICA BY KIPE OFFSET PROCESS CO., INC., NEW YORK

CONTENTS

LET'S GO TO THE DESERT

There are many little animals and plants to see.

Some of the animals are hard to find.

But they are worth looking for

because they are so interesting.

MOUNTAINS AND CLOUDS

A desert is a land

where there is scarcely any water or rain.

The air is dry and the earth is dry.

You can see in the picture the mountains and rain clouds.

The clouds leave their moisture or rain on the mountains.

The wind which has brought the clouds

from the ocean becomes dry and warm

as it blows down the mountainside into the desert.

2

DESERT WASH

When it does rain the water comes tumbling
down the mountainsides.
This water runs into little creeks
which grow into larger creeks or rivers
at the foot of the mountain.
After the rain is over,
the water sinks into the ground.
Then all we can see is where
the water has washed the sand away.
Sometimes under the sand of the wash
there is water.

CREOSOTE BUSH

After a rain the plants grow
and store every drop of water they can.
Different plants have different ways
of keeping this water or sap from evaporating
or drying up during the hot summer months.
Some plants have tiny, shiny leaves—
like the creosote bush.
These leaves are covered with a gummy substance
which keeps the sap from oozing out
and then evaporating into the air.
This bush is called a creosote bush
because it smells like creosote.

There are many creosote bushes in the desert.

They grow to be taller than you.

Or even taller than your father and mother.

In the spring the bushes are covered

with little yellow flowers.

From these flowers woolly white seed pods develop.

They make the bush look as though it were covered

with little pieces of white cotton.

The seeds are blown to the ground.

The sand is blown over them.

In spring the rain helps the seeds

to grow into other creosote bushes.

OCOTILLO

Some plants have tiny, delicate leaves
on hard stems or stalks—like the ocotillo.
The leaves come in the springtime.
During the hot and dry months
the leaves dry up and fall off.
The bushes grow to be from about
ten to twenty feet tall.
Most bushes in the desert have long roots.
These roots reach or grow way down under the sand
for tiny drops of water that are in the ground.

The ocotillo's flowers are red.

They grow along the end of each stalk.

Seen from far away,

they look like the flame of a candle.

The seeds drop to the ground.

They are covered with sand.

The rains come and later other ocotillo bushes grow.

But not all the seeds grow into other bushes,

for birds and little animals eat them.

And quite often it doesn't rain enough.

12

PALO VERDE

Some plants are covered with powder,

like the palo verde tree.

Palo verde means green tree in Spanish.

The tree is called palo verde

because it always has green branches and trunks.

They are covered with a light green powder.

This powder helps to prevent or stop

any water or sap from evaporating.

14

A palo verde when it is little has leaves.

When it is grown up it has thorns.

Only in springtime does it have leaves.

In the picture you can see

how delicate are the tiny leaves.

A palo verde tree's flower looks like

a small yellow pea blossom.

They have a perfume like sweet-pea blossoms.

Like pea blossoms, they turn into seed pods.

Not many little palo verde trees grow up

because there is not enough water every year.

In fact, palo verde trees almost always grow in sandy washes,

or in places where there is water underground.

Palo verde trees usually grow from ten to twenty feet high.

Palo verde trees live ten to twenty years.

SMOKE TREE

Smoke trees are called smoke trees

because from far away

they look like a puff of smoke.

They are the color of smoke—gray.

Their branches are really green

but are covered with a whitish powder.

That is why a smoke tree is sometimes also called

a palo blanco or white tree.

A smoke tree is very much like a palo verde tree.

They both have thorns and leaves only in springtime.

They both are covered with a powder.

They both live near sandy washes.

They both have a pealike blossom

which develops into a seed pod.

The smoke tree's blossom is dark blue.

Smoke trees usually grow from ten to twenty feet high.

And live ten to twenty years.

BARREL CACTUS

Some plants have no leaves

but only stems—like the cactus.

The barrel cactus has one stem or body.

It is called a barrel cactus

because it is round like a barrel.

The barrel cactus keeps its water or sap inside its body.

This is helpful to thirsty animals

that can gnaw a hole into the cactus and get the water or sap.

This doesn't harm the cactus

because it can grow another skin to cover the hole.

Of course the cactus protects itself with many thorns.

These thorns are colored pink, red and white.

A barrel cactus's body is green.

The flowers of the barrel cactus

blossom on its top.

They form a circle, like a crown.

Some barrel cactuses' blossoms are red.

The blossoms develop into seeds.

CHOLLA CACTUS

All cactuses have prickles or thorns to protect them.

Some prickles are tiny, like the hair on your arm.

Some prickles are the size of a pin or larger.

Some have small, curved ends.

Some have sharp points.

In this picture the cholla's prickles

or thorns gleam and glisten in the sunlight—

like a soft yellow fuzz.

But if you have ever been pricked

you know that their points hurt badly.

A cholla cactus has bad thorns.

They stick quickly into whatever touches them.

In the picture you can see the cholla fruit.

Although the cactus's skin is tough

and covered with thorns and prickles—

its flowers are as delicate as a lily.

Some cactuses grow from seeds,

like the barrel cactus.

Some cactuses grow from joints,

like the cholla cactus.

The joints fall off onto the ground.

Into the ground grow roots.

Into the air grows another joint.

From this joint grows another joint,

and so another cactus grows.

A cholla grows about as fast as you—

six inches a year.

Some chollas are about as tall as you, three or four feet.

Some chollas grow as high as eight or twelve feet.

PRICKLY-PEAR CACTUS

The prickly-pear cactus is called a prickly pear

because its fruit is shaped or tastes like a pear.

Sometimes it is called beaver-tail cactus

because its joints are flat and shaped

like the tail of a beaver.

It has no thorns, but on the joints

are bunches of small, thin prickles.

These are hard to get out of your skin.

The prickly pear grows from joints,

like the cholla cactus.

Its blossoms are like the cholla's—only pinkish.

Its fruit turns orange when it is ripe.

Then you can eat it or make it into candy.

Some kinds of prickly pears grow in bunches

about a foot high.

Other kinds grow to be from ten to fifteen feet high.

They live for many years.

SAGUARO CACTUS

A saguaro cactus looks as though it were stretching

its arms up to the sky.

Some birds like to make holes in these arms.

In these holes the birds make their nests.

There are some nest holes in the left arm of the saguaro in the picture.

Saguaro cactuses grow to be about thirty feet high.

We cannot always tell the age of a plant by its size.

Some years there is more water than other years.

And cactus plants grow faster when they have water.

Saguaro cactuses grow to be very old, perhaps a hundred or more years.

A saguaro's blossom grows at the end

of each arm—like the barrel cactus.

The blossoms are waxy white and about the size of an Easter lily.

These blossoms turn into fruit with seeds inside.

When the fruit drops to the ground and dries,

some of the seeds are covered by sand.

The rains come and the seeds grow.

30

JOSHUA TREE

A Joshua tree is not a cactus or a palm tree.

A Joshua tree is a lily plant, the biggest of all.

The points of the silver-green leaves

are needle sharp.

Joshua trees grow on the hillsides,

where they can get more water

than down in the desert.

A Joshua tree keeps its sap inside its trunk.

Some Joshua trees grow to be thirty feet high.

32

Some Joshua trees grow to be

many, many hundreds of years old.

A Joshua tree's flowers grow in bunches

at the ends of the branches or arms.

They are greenish-yellowish white.

The blossoms are like a lily bud.

They open into bell-shaped flowers.

SAND DUNES

In some places the desert is covered with sand.

This sand is gathered or blown by the wind

into piles—called dunes.

On these dunes the wind leaves

the sand in ripples.

In some places the sand is almost white,

and when the sun shines on it,

it glistens like snow.

In other places the sand is red,

brown, gray or greenish gray.

36

In the spring, after a few rains,

the sand is covered with flowers.

They make the desert look as though it were covered

with a yellow, white and purple carpet.

During the winter the seeds lie in the sand.

In the spring the rains and sun make the seeds grow.

The flowers bloom and look beautiful for a few weeks.

Then the blossoms turn into seeds,

which again lie in the sand and wait until the next spring

to blossom forth and make another carpet of flowers.   38

LIZARDS

When a lizard rests he usually

holds his head and shoulders up.

His hind legs are bent and ready,

so that he can run away immediately.

Some lizards run so fast

you can scarcely see them go.

Some snakes and birds like to eat lizards.

Lizards have several ways of protecting themselves.

Usually they trust to their fast legs

to escape from their enemies.

Sometimes they bury themselves in the sand.

Some lizards' tails break off easily.

This is convenient, for if a lizard's tail is caught,

the tail is left in his enemy's grasp.

Later the lizard grows another tail.

A lizard's skin is covered with small scales.

Some lizards are spotted brown, yellow,

gray, tan, black, red or green.

Some lizards look very much like the color

of the sand or plants where they live.

In winter a lizard sleeps in the sand or under rocks.

In the summer, during the hot part of the day,

he crawls under some cactus or rocks.

There are many kinds of lizards.

Some kinds of lizards eat insects. Some lizards eat plants.

Some lizards eat other lizards.

And, sad to say, some lizards eat their own babies.

Some mother lizards lay their eggs under rocks and sticks.

Other mother lizards bury them in the sand.

Some mothers lay six eggs,

while other mothers lay twenty or more.

Some eggs are the size of a pea and some are much larger.

Lizards may live for eight years.

CHUCKAWALLAS

A chuckawalla is also a lizard.

He is larger than the common lizards.

In fact, he is about a foot long.

He is colored brown with reddish spots.

Sometimes his stomach is salmon pink.

His tail is light tan with bands of brown.

When he is in the shade—his color is dark brown.

When he is in the sunlight—his color is light tan.

It takes a little time for him to change his color.

His four short legs are sturdy.

He can run fast but not as fast as the small lizards.

In winter he sleeps in between rocks.

In summer he likes to lie on the hot rocks—

unless they are too hot.

A chuckawalla has a flat body,

but when he is scared he puffs or blows himself up.

When he is in between rocks and he has blown himself up

he cannot be pulled out by a bird or snake.

He has another way of protecting himself.

He can use his tail like a whip.

Chuckawallas play together.

They peep around rocks, catch hold

of each other's tails—like kittens at play.

They also fight each other.

When a chuckawalla is frightened he will open his mouth.

Like most lizards, he has tiny teeth.

He can and will bite to defend himself.

A chuckawalla eats leaves and flowers.

The mother chuckawalla lays her six eggs in the sand.

Baby chuckawallas are about three inches long.

Chuckawallas may live to be eight years old.

HORNED TOADS

A horned toad isn't a toad at all, but a lizard.

He has been called a toad

because his body is about the size of a toad's.

He has been called horned

because his head is covered with hornlike spines.

Unless an animal is very, very hungry,

it will not eat a horned toad,

because the prickly spines would hurt its throat.

A horned toad can run fast

but not for more than a few feet.

Usually he escapes his enemies

by running under bushes or burrowing in the sand.

When he burrows he starts to dig with his head.

This he turns swiftly from side to side,

using it as a shovel and lever—

and in he slides under the sand.

In winter a horned toad digs himself

in the sand to go to sleep.

When spring comes he crawls out of the sand.

While he was asleep his body was cold and stiff.

To warm himself he lies on the warm sand or rocks.

If you tickle a horned toad under his chin

or on top of his head, he will lie quietly.

In fact, you might think he was asleep.

When a horned toad catches ants and other insects

he stands on tiptoe on his front feet.

He excitedly moves his head and body up and down.

His tail twitches.

When the insect is close enough

the horned toad's sticky tongue darts out—

the insect is stuck to the tongue

and swallowed in one gulp—for he has no teeth.

A horned toad is spotted brown and gray.

His color is his protection.

If you take a quick look at this picture

you might think it was only sandy earth,

for a horned toad looks like the desert ground.

Some mother horned toads lay eggs in the sand.

Other mother horned toads keep their eggs

inside their body until after they are hatched.

Mother horned toads have about twenty-four babies.

The babies are only half an inch or an inch long.

Horned toads live about eight years.

SCORPIONS

Desert scorpions are light amber color.

Amber looks like brownish-orange glass.

This color is not a protection,

as is the color of lizards and snakes.

During the winter and in the hot summer

a scorpion hides under rocks

or buries himself in the sand.

A scorpion has eight legs and two pinchers.

He carries his stinger at the end of his tail.

A scorpion stings to kill his food.

It eats insects and spiders.

A scorpion is about the size

of the one in the picture.

To sting, the scorpion must lift
his tail over his head.
With his two pinchers he holds onto
whatever he wishes to sting.
Then he strikes down with his tail
and his stinger goes into the tiny animal.
A sting from a desert scorpion is not dangerous,
but it hurts much more than a bee's sting.
A scorpion does not lose
his stinger like a bee.

This is a big picture of a scorpion.

You can see his mouth parts.

They look like extra arms.

The mother scorpion keeps her eggs

inside her body until they are ready to hatch.

Then she carries the tiny babies

around with her on her back,

her tail up—ready to protect them.

You can imagine how tiny the babies are

when you know that there are over a hundred of them.

A scorpion usually lives two or three years.

TARANTULAS

A tarantula is a large brown or black spider.

In this picture of a tarantula you can see his mouth

and the two shiny, poisonous fangs.

Like a spider, he has eight legs.

What you might think are extra legs are a kind of arm.

They are mouth parts which help

the tarantula to hold its food.

A tarantula eats insects and other spiders.

His eight eyes cannot see things.

They can only tell the difference

between shade and sunlight.

A tarantula doesn't like very hot sunlight.

He does most of his hunting or waiting for food at night.

When an insect comes close enough to touch the tarantula,

out go his front legs to grab the insect.

A tarantula's bite kills the insect immediately,

but hurts a grownup no more than a scorpion's sting.

The mother tarantulas make their homes

in holes or under rocks.

The mother tarantula lays about

a hundred eggs in a silken cocoon.

This cocoon is almost as large as she is.

She rolls out her eggs to give them a sunbath.

When the babies are grown up enough

they come out of the cocoon.

They are about the size of a scorpion's babies.

Tarantulas may live two or three years.

TRADE OR PACK RATS

The trade rat is called a trade rat, or a pack rat,

because people think it trades things.

It doesn't really trade.

If it is carrying one thing

and sees another thing it likes better,

it will drop the one it is carrying

and pick up the new thing.

Trade rats like shiny things.

Many spoons, knives and can openers

have been taken by trade rats.

In their place is usually left a rock,

piece of wood or cactus.

A trade rat has large ears

and big, bright eyes.

Its smooth fur is colored grayish tan.

Its stomach and paws are colored white.

The trade rat likes to run about at night.

He gathers seeds and green plants.

But best of all he likes to eat—cactuses.

A trade rat's home is a mound

of sticks and stones.

The entrances are usually protected

on the outside with cactus joints.

Inside there are many passages and rooms.

These rooms are usually spotlessly clean.

In one room the rat keeps his food.

Another is the nursery for the baby rats.

This the mother rat has lined

with soft grass and some of her fur.

A mother rat is very good to her two babies.

She lets them play and crawl all over her,

and she takes them everywhere she goes.

Trade rats may live to be six years old.

KANGAROO RATS

Kangaroo rats are called kangaroo rats
because they look like a kangaroo.
They have long hind legs, a long tail
and short front legs.
Like a kangaroo, the rat hops about.
Usually he makes little short hops,
but if he is frightened, he can leap a foot or two.
And, like a kangaroo, the rat uses his tail
to help support or balance himself when he hops
or when he sits back on his hind legs.
He uses his front paws as hands.
The kangaroo rat has a pocket on either side of his face.
In these pockets he carries seeds.
When he gets home he takes the seeds
out of the pockets and puts them in the storeroom.
A kangaroo rat makes his home or burrow in the sand.

A kangaroo rat doesn't drink much water.

But if he is very thirsty

he will gnaw into a barrel cactus.

His fur is tannish gray and white.

The tip of his tail is tufted.

Sometimes, if he is frightened,

he will thump his tail up and down.

Perhaps this is to warn other rats

that there is an enemy near.

He likes to hunt and play at night.

The mother kangaroo rat has two, four or six babies.

Kangaroo rats live to be about three or four years old.

RATTLESNAKES

Some snakes in the desert are harmless—

but some are dangerous.

One dangerous snake, called the desert diamondback,

warns you that he is near.

He wriggles his tail,

which makes a rattling, buzzing sound.

This is because at its end

there are some roundish scales.

These scales make a rattling sound when shaken.

The more excited the snake becomes,

the faster his tail rattles shake.

That is why he is called a rattlesnake.

We can pretend that the rattles say,

"Run, runnie, run, whirr—buzz.

Run before I bite, whirr, buzz."

During the winter, and when it is hot,

rattlesnakes hide under rocks.

In fact, a rattlesnake would die

if he stayed in the hot sunlight for more than an hour.

When asleep or resting,

a snake winds himself up in circles or coils.

If you tease or poke a snake,

it will defend itself by trying to bite you.

To bite you, the snake must be coiled

so it can thrust its head toward you.

This is called striking.

A rattlesnake can strike about one third its length.

Rattlesnakes grow to be about four or six feet long.

A snake's tongue is forked or divided in two at the end.

It is often quivering in and out,

because it is the snake's smeller.

He has two nostrils through which he breathes.

These are in the front part of his head.

In a rattlesnake's mouth are two teeth or fangs.

They are about half the length of a pin.

In the picture you can see these fangs.

They are on the roof of the snake's mouth.

They are covered with skin except at the points.

They are connected to poison sacs—

one on each side of the snake's head.

When the snake bites, the poison squirts out

through a hole at the point of the fang—

into the flesh of the snake's enemy.

Rattlesnakes eat lizards, rats and rabbits.

The mother rattlesnake keeps her eggs

inside her body until they are hatched.

She has about seventy-five babies.

Some rattlesnakes live to be fourteen years old.

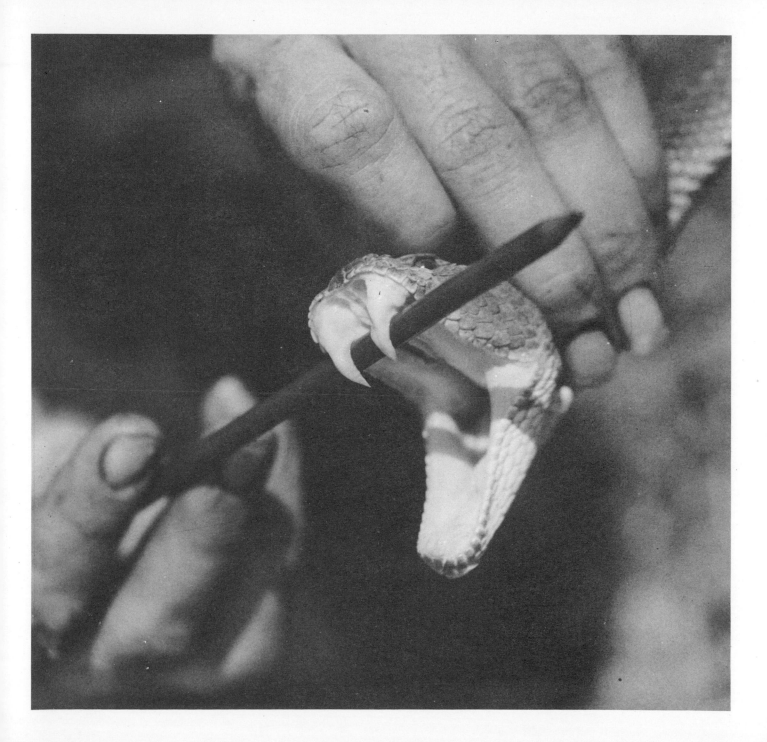

SIDEWINDERS

There is another dangerous snake in the desert.

It is a rattlesnake called a sidewinder.

He is called a sidewinder because he crawls

to the side instead of straight ahead.

He winds his body into an S.

A sidewinder can move fast.

But he couldn't catch you if you ran.

He is afraid of you.

If you strike or hurt him,

then he tries to bite you to protect himself.

But you probably won't meet him,

because he usually moves about at night,

looking for rats and mice to eat.

In the daytime he hides under bushes from the hot sun.   80

A sidewinder is twelve or more inches long.

A sidewinder lives on the sandy parts of the desert.

He is sand color with tan spots.

About twice a year, like all snakes,

a sidewinder sheds his skin.

His new skin has been growing for several months.

The old skin splits open at the top of his head.

Then the sidewinder wriggles out of his old skin.

This takes about half an hour.

The mother sidewinder keeps her eggs

inside her until they are hatched.

She has about fifteen or more babies.

Sidewinders live to be about fifteen years old

DESERT TORTOISES

A desert tortoise walks like an elephant,

slowly, heavily and clumsily.

His head wobbles up and down, as though he were saying,

"Yes, yes, yes. I know all about it,

for I'm very old. I'm probably older

than your father. Yes, yes, yes."

The tortoise has a gentle nature.

He looks wise because of his bright eyes and his wrinkled skin.

His shell is brown on top and yellowish on its underside.

A tortoise's legs are covered with smooth scales.

His front feet have four claws.

His hind feet have five claws.

Don't think that because a tortoise is big

he is older than a small tortoise.

It is the amount of food a tortoise can get that makes him grow.

Some lucky tortoises grow to be about a foot long.

Of course they are old, perhaps fifty years old. 84

Like many desert animals, a tortoise doesn't often drink.

A tortoise has two water sacs inside his body.

There he stores away his water supply.

Sometimes he drinks dewdrops.

Once or twice a year he will take a drink

from a rain puddle.

A tortoise hasn't any teeth.

His jaws are notched like a saw.

He bites off what he wants to eat.

His pinkish tongue licks off any pieces

that are stuck to the sides of his jaws.

When it is very hot the tortoise

eats and moves about only at night.

In the daytime he will hide in a hole.

In the spring the mother tortoise lays her eggs.

After three months in the sun-warmed sand,

these eggs hatch into baby.tortoises.

The mother tortoise lays from two to six eggs.

In winter a tortoise crawls into a hole.

He doesn't pull in his legs and head when he sleeps.

Like you, he gets comfortable,

relaxes and shuts his eyes.

He will wake up only if it is warm.

Of course he will pull in his head and legs

if he has to protect himself.

When he shuts himself up in his shell—he hisses.

This hissing isn't because he is angry or frightened.

It is only that there isn't enough room

inside his shell for his body

and the air in his lungs too—

so, "whuuuuuuiissss" goes the air.